A PRIMARY SOURCE HISTORY OF THE UNITED STATES

AN EMERGING WORLD POWER

1900–1929

George E. Stanley

WORLD ALMANAC® LIBRARY

★ ★ ★

Please visit our web site at: www.worldalmanaclibrary.com
For a free color catalog describing World Almanac® Library's list of high-quality
books and multimedia programs, call 1-800-848-2928 (USA) or 1-800-387-3178
(Canada). World Almanac® Library's fax: (414) 332-3567.

Library of Congress Cataloging-in-Publication Data available upon request from publisher.
Fax (414) 336-0157 for the attention of the Publishing Records Department.

ISBN 0-8368-5828-X (lib. bdg.)
ISBN 0-8368-5837-9 (softcover)

First published in 2005 by
World Almanac® Library
330 West Olive Street, Suite 100
Milwaukee, WI 53212 USA

Copyright © 2005 by World Almanac® Library.

Produced by Byron Preiss Visual Publications Inc.
Project Editor: Susan Hoe
Designer: Marisa Gentile
World Almanac® Library editor: Alan Wachtel
World Almanac® Library art direction: Tammy West

Picture acknowledgements:
clipart.com: Cover (upper right). The Granger Collection, New York: Cover (upper left,
lower left, lower right), p. 42. Library of Congress: pp. 5, 6, 7, 8, 9, 10, 11, 13, 15,
17, 19, 21, 23, 24, 27, 28, 31, 33, 34, 37, 38.

Printed in the United States of America

1 2 3 4 5 6 7 8 9 09 08 07 06 05

Dr. George E. Stanley is a professor at Cameron University in Lawton, Oklahoma. He has authored
more than eighty books for young readers, many in the field of history and science. Dr. Stanley recently
completed a series of history books on famous Americans, including *Geronimo, Andrew Jackson,
Harry S. Truman,* and *Mr. Rogers.*

CONTENTS

Through the examination of authentic historical documents, including charters, diaries, journals, letters, speeches, and other written records, each title in *A Primary Source History of the United States* offers a unique perspective on the events that shaped the United States. In addition to providing important historical information, each document serves as a piece of living history that opens a window into the kinds of thinking and modes of expression that characterized the various epochs of American history.

Note: To facilitate the reading of older documents, the modern-day spelling of certain words is used.

CHAPTER 1

The Progressive Movement

1900–1913

It was the start of a new century and the United States had emerged from the semi-isolation of the nineteenth century to become a world power. During what was known as the "Progressive Era"— around 1900–1920—the United States government tried to respond to the problems caused by industrialization and urbanization. Urban, middle-class Americans wanted the government to have a larger role in addressing such issues as the control of big business and public welfare.

Although a Progressive political party was formed in 1912, the movement also had wide support from both Democrats and Republicans. Presidents Theodore Roosevelt, William Taft, and Woodrow Wilson all claimed to be "progressives."

On September 6, 1901, President William McKinley was shot by an unemployed millworker, and Vice President Theodore Roosevelt became the president. Roosevelt wanted the government to take a greater role in public welfare. He believed that enforcement of the Sherman Antitrust Act (passed by Congress in 1890) would be a good first step toward this, and he often gave speeches on the need to curtail the power of corporate trusts.

ROOSEVELT'S MUSIC HALL SPEECH: 1902

… While making it clear that we do not intend to allow wrongdoing by one of the captains of industry any more than by the humblest private in the industrial ranks, we must also in the interests of all of us avoid cramping a strength which, if beneficently used, will be for the good of all of us…. In securing just and fair dealing by these men let us remember to do them justice in return….

SOCIAL PROBLEMS

Writers were often the first to make citizens aware of the problems in society. The muckrakers, as they were known, exposed municipal corruption and ruthless business practices. Their impact could be powerful, as in the case of Upton Sinclair's novel *The Jungle*, published in 1906. Its vivid description of unsanitary conditions in the meatpacking plants of Chicago led directly to federal laws regulating several industries and products.

▲ A photograph, c.1902, of Roosevelt delivering a speech in Massachusetts.

CHAPTER 7 OF SINCLAIR'S *THE JUNGLE*: 1906

... There was no heat upon the killing beds.... For that matter, there was very little heat anywhere in the building.... On the killing beds you were apt to be covered with blood, and it would freeze solid; if you leaned against a pillar, you would freeze to that, and if you put your hand upon the blade of your knife, you would run a chance of leaving your skin on it.... Now and then, when the bosses were not looking, you would see them [the men workers] plunging their feet and ankles into the steaming hot carcass of the steer.... The cruelest thing of all was that nearly all of them ... who used knives ... were unable to wear gloves, and their arms would be white with frost and their hands would grow numb, and then of course there would be accidents....

— ★ —

Congress passed the Meat Inspection Act, which allowed the government to condemn any meat found unfit for human consumption. Congress also passed the Pure Food and Drug Act, which forbade the manufacture, sale, or transport of impure food products or poisonous patent medicines.

PROGRESSIVE LABOR LAWS

Progressives, such as the members of the National Child Labor Committee, coordinated a movement to address the problems of children working long hours under terrible conditions. Some of the committee's most effective weapons were photographs that showed boys and girls as young as eight years old working with dangerous equipment in coal mines and factories.

By 1910, many states had already enacted legislation that established the maximum length of a workday or workweek and the minimum legal age when children could work, but even these varied from state to state. Many parents who needed the income from their child's labor would

OREGON STATE SESSION LAWS: 1903

... No female [shall] be employed in any mechanical establishment, or factory, or laundry in this state more than ten hours during any one day. The hours of work may be so arranged as to permit the employment of females at any time so that they shall not work more than ten hours during the twenty-four hours of any one day....

also lie about their child's age. Gradually, the number of children working decreased, although whether it was because of the labor laws or because of the new state laws requiring school attendance is difficult to determine.

Progressives also wanted to limit how long women could work. They argued that long hours in a factory were harmful to a woman's well-being. In 1908, the Supreme Court agreed in *Muller* v. *Oregon* and upheld a state law

▲ Children marching in a 1909 labor parade in New York City carry signs in English and in Yiddish equating child labor with slavery.

that limited women working in laundries to no more than ten hours a day. This case was significant because, by its ruling, the court accepted the Brandeis Brief (submitted by attorney Louis Brandeis), which was the sociological, economic, and medical evidence that showed a woman's health was impaired by long factory hours.

Unfortunately, some changes in working conditions came only as a result of tragedy. On March 25, 1911, almost one hundred fifty workers, mostly teenage Italian and Jewish immigrant girls, died in the Triangle Shirtwaist Company fire when they were trapped in locked workrooms and couldn't escape. The only "escape measure" was a fire escape that collapsed under the weight of the panic-stricken workers. When the horse-drawn fire engine arrived at the burning building, they discovered that the ladders were two floors too short.

The public outcry from this terrible event led to investigations and legislation that changed almost every aspect of the factory conditions in New York State. Besides imposing new building regulations, the legislature established a shorter workweek for women and barred children under fourteen years of age from working.

◀ This photograph taken on March 25, 1911, shows a horse-drawn fire engine racing to the Triangle Shirtwaist Company fire.

CONSERVATION AWARENESS

Many Americans believed that the supply of new lands and natural resources in the United States was unlimited, but in 1890, the government announced that a western frontier no longer existed.

A bitter debate followed, which continues today, between those who argued that the United States should exploit its natural resources as long as they last and those who favored conservation as a means to sustain supply over a longer period of time and to preserve the land's natural beauty.

Theodore Roosevelt, a sportsman and a naturalist, sided emphatically with the conservationists. He supported legislation that would change the way America used its land, especially in the West. The Newlands Act of 1902 gave the federal government an active role in the areas of water management and reclamation.

President Roosevelt also worked to preserve more than 230 million acres of land in the form of national parks and monuments. He continually addressed the subject of conservation in speeches he gave around the nation.

ROOSEVELT'S SPEECH ON THE REDWOOD TREES: 1903

... Yesterday I saw for the first time a grove of your great trees [redwoods], a grove which it has taken the ages several thousands of years to build up; and I felt most emphatically that we should not turn into shingles a tree which was old when the first Egyptian conqueror penetrated to the valley of the Euphrates, which it has taken so many thousands of years to build up, and which can be put to better use....

▲ This photograph, c.1903, shows Roosevelt and others in front of some redwood trees in California.

INNOVATION AND EXPLORATION IN THE PROGRESSIVE ERA

Advances in technology and exploration also occurred during the Progressive Era. There was something about the spirit of this era coupled with the beginning of a new century that brought out the creative genius in some Americans. Wilbur and Orville Wright spent several years building flying machines in their Dayton, Ohio, bicycle shop.

Their work paid off on December 17, 1903, at Kitty Hawk, North Carolina. Orville piloted the gasoline-powered airplane, staying in the air for fifty-nine seconds and traveling

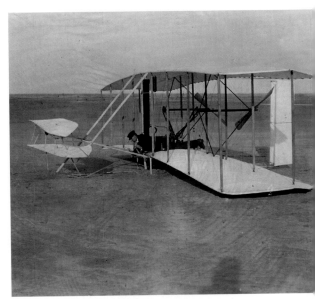

▲ A photograph of Wilbur Wright in his damaged flying machine after an unsuccessful trial run on December 14, 1903.

TELEGRAM TO THE WRIGHTS' FATHER: 1903

Kitty Hawk NC Dec 17
Bishop M Wright
7 Hawthorne St
Success four flights Thursday morning all against twenty one mile wind started from Level with engine power alone average speed through air thirty one miles longest 57 seconds inform Press.... Orevell Wright....

120 feet. Afterward, he sent his father, Milton, a telegram informing him of their success, but the telegraph operator made a mistake in the length of the flight and also misspelled Orville's name.

For many other Americans, the era rekindled a sense of adventure and a desire to go where no one had ever gone before.

Robert Peary, a civil engineer with the U.S. Navy, had already made several trips to Greenland to survey that island when he announced in 1897 that he planned a daring expedition to the North Pole. Although that attempt and another one in 1905 were unsuccessful, Peary's fame grew and garnered him an invitation to speak on the thrill of exploration at New York's exclusive Lotus Club.

Two years after he delivered this speech, Peary, his assistant Matthew Henson, and four Eskimo aides inched their way northward until on April 6, 1909, they stood on the North Pole.

Through his trips to the Arctic, Peary helped contribute to the scientific knowledge of glacial formations and to the development of a system of Arctic travel that future explorers could use.

PEARY'S SPEECH TO THE LOTUS CLUB IN NEW YORK: 1907

... The discovery not only of the North, but of the South Pole as well, is not only our privilege but our duty and destiny.... The discovery of the poles spells ... national prestige, with the moral strength that comes from the feeling that not even century-defying problems can withstand us....

◄ Robert Peary shows the type of fur clothing he wore when he reached the North Pole in 1909.

THE PANAMA CANAL

The United States became a world power, with possessions stretching halfway around the world, from the Caribbean to the Pacific, when it acquired Puerto Rico, Guam, and the Philippines from Spain after the Spanish-American War in 1898–99. Because the war had been fought in both the Atlantic and the Pacific, the United States realized that a link between the two oceans would save travel time.

In the 1880s, the French had tried but failed to build a canal across the Isthmus of Panama, so the United States decided to take over the project. In 1903, the Hay-Herran Treaty was signed with Colombia. At the

HAY-BUNAU-VARILLA TREATY: 1903

... The United States guarantees and will maintain the independence of the Republic of Panama.

The Republic of Panama grants to the United States in perpetuity the use, occupation and control of a zone of land and land under water for the construction, maintenance, operation, sanitation, and protection of [a] Canal of the width of ten miles extending to the distance of five miles on each side of the center line of the route of the Canal to be constructed....

▲ A photograph taken of the SS *Panama* taking the first excursion through the Panama Canal in 1914.

time, Panama was a province of Colombia. However, the Colombian legislature rejected the treaty.

Panamanian revolutionists revolted, and the United States immediately recognized the new government. On November 18, 1903, they negotiated the Hay-Bunau-Varilla Treaty with Panama, which gave them the right to build and operate a canal that was ten miles long.

Construction on the canal began in 1904. Tens of thousands of workers sweated in the malarial heat and battled the disease-carrying mosquitoes. They tore up jungles and cut down mountains. Still, they were able to build a railroad, three sets of concrete locks—which were used to raise and lower the water levels for the ships—and an artificial lake. On August 15, 1914, the first ship passed through the canal. By using the Panama Canal, a ship traveling from New York City to San Francisco could save almost eight thousand travel miles.

While the canal construction was a major feat of engineering, medical advances that occurred during the ten-year period, such as the eradication of yellow fever and better control over malaria and other tropical diseases, were important accomplishments, as well.

CHAPTER 2

Wilson and World War I

1913–1918

In 1904, the government of the Dominican Republic went bankrupt, and President Theodore Roosevelt feared that Germany and other European nations might intervene forcibly to collect their debts. On December 6, as part of his annual message to Congress, he issued the Roosevelt Corollary to the Monroe Doctrine, which he and later American presidents would cite to justify United States intervention in the nations of the Caribbean and Central America.

ROOSEVELT'S ANNUAL MESSAGE TO CONGRESS: 1904

... All this country desires is to see the neighboring countries [in the Western Hemisphere] stable, orderly, and prosperous. Any country whose people conduct themselves well can count upon our hearty friendship ... [and] need fear no interference from the United States. Chronic wrongdoing [however] ... may force the United States ... to the exercise of an international police power....

WOODROW WILSON TAKES OFFICE

After the 1904 election, Theodore Roosevelt announced that he would not run again. Four years later, William Howard Taft, Roosevelt's handpicked successor, defeated Democrat William Jennings Bryan. Taft continued Roosevelt's policies of reform. In 1912, Roosevelt indicated that he would accept the presidential nomination if it were offered, but Republican conservatives made sure that Taft was the party's candidate. Roosevelt and his followers bolted and formed the Progressive party.

The Democrats nominated Woodrow Wilson, the governor of New Jersey. Wilson easily won the election, which brought the Democrats back to power for the first time since the Civil War.

The party now controlled the White House and both houses of Congress. True to his promise, President Wilson got Congress to pass the Underwood-Simmons Tariff Act, which was the first law in more than fifty years to lower taxes on imported goods. Products that were no longer charged duties now included iron, steel, raw wood, and sugar. To make up for the reduced government income, the tariff law implemented the federal income tax, as permitted by the Sixteenth Amendment. It levied a one percent tax on all incomes over $4,000, and went up accordingly with higher incomes.

SIXTEENTH AMENDMENT: 1913

The Congress shall have power to lay and collect taxes on incomes, from whatever course derived, without apportionment among the several States, and without regard to any census or enumeration.

Of all of Wilson's domestic programs, the reorganization of the nation's banking system was the most important. At that time, most of the money in the United States was controlled by a handful of eastern banks, so Wilson asked Congress to pass the Federal Reserve Act, which set up twelve federal reserve banks in regions across the country. Under the supervision of the Federal Reserve Board, these district banks would lend money to member banks in their area at a low interest rate. Lower interest rates also tended to stimulate business, by making more money available for expansion.

▲ This portrait of Woodrow Wilson, twenty-eighth president of the United States, was taken between 1900 and 1920.

ANTITRUST LEGISLATION

The cornerstone of President Wilson's antitrust policy was the Federal Trade Commission, which was established in 1914. Its purpose was to control deceptive advertising and mislabeling of containers in interstate commerce. Already existing antitrust laws were strengthened with the passage of the Clayton Antitrust Act, which outlawed such business practices as price discrimination—that is, selling products so low that other, usually smaller, stores would go out of business. This act also allowed workers to strike, and

THE CLAYTON ANTITRUST ACT: 1914

... It shall be unlawful for any person engaged in commerce, in the course of such commerce, either directly or indirectly, to discriminate in price between different purchasers of commodities of like grade and quality ... where such commodities are sold for use, consumption, or resale within the United States or any Territory thereof or the District of Columbia or any ... possession or other place under the jurisdiction of the United States....

— ★ —

injunctions against strikes were prohibited most of the time. Unfortunately, the degree of protection from management retaliation, which these provisions actually offered unions, depended on court interpretations. Sometimes strike issues led to bloodshed.

Coal miners in Colorado wanted to unionize by joining the United Mine Workers of America, but the Colorado Fuel and Iron Company bitterly opposed this. In Ludlow, Colorado, on April 20, 1914, Colorado militia, coal company guards, and strikebreakers killed twenty men, women, and children who had been evicted from their company-owned houses and had set up a tent colony on public property. Folk singer Woody Guthrie wrote a song about the massacre.

◀ Striking coal miners, who worked long hours for low wages, toiled in cramped, sweltering mines. They were under the constant threat of cave-ins and breathed in coal dust, which often caused major health problems.

"LUDLOW MASSACRE" BY WOODY GUTHRIE: 1944

It was early springtime that the strike was on
They moved us miners out of door
Out from the houses that the company owned
We moved into tents at old Ludlow....

That very night you soldiers waited
Until us miners were asleep
You snuck around our little tent town
Soaked our tent with your kerosene

You struck a match and the blaze it started
You pulled the triggers of your Gatling guns
I made a run for the children but the fire wall stopped me
Thirteen children died from your guns....

66 You pulled the triggers of your Gatling guns... 99

Start of World War I in Europe

On June 28, 1914, Archduke Franz Ferdinand, heir to the throne of Austria-Hungary, was assassinated by a Serbian nationalist in Sarajevo. The Serbian government denied any involvement with the murder, but when Austria threatened to retaliate anyway, Serbia turned to its ally, Russia, for help. When Russia began to mobilize its army, Austria's ally, Germany, declared war on Russia and France, which was also Russia's ally. Great Britain entered the war on August 4, following Germany's invasion of neutral Belgium. By the end of August, most of Europe had chosen sides. President Wilson quickly proclaimed America's neutrality.

DECLARATION OF NEUTRALITY: 1914

The effect of the war upon the United States will depend upon what American citizens say and do. Every man who really loves America will act and speak in the true spirit of neutrality, which is the spirit of impartiality and fairness and friendliness to all concerned. The spirit of the nation in this critical matter will be determined largely by what individuals and society and those gathered in public meetings do and say, upon what newspaper and magazines contain, upon what ministers utter in their pulpits, and men proclaim ... upon the street....

Sinking of the Lusitania

In May 1915, the British ocean liner *Lusitania* was sunk by German submarines. Among the dead were one hundred twenty-eight Americans. Although many people demanded that the United States go to war, President Wilson persuaded Germany to abandon its attacks on commercial ships, but he decided that it would be prudent to take the necessary steps to get the country ready for war if it came. The National Defense Act provided for the expansion of the regular army, and the Naval Construction Act called for a building program for the navy. The Council of National Defense

WILSON'S SPEECH ON THE SUSSEX CASE: 1916

... I have deemed it my duty ... to say to the Imperial German Government ... that unless ... [it] ... should now immediately declare and effect an abandonment of its present methods of warfare against passenger and freight carrying vessels this Government can have no choice but to sever diplomatic relations with the Government of the German Empire altogether....

mobilized industry, available natural resources, and labor in the event of a war with Germany.

In March 1916, the French steamer *Sussex* was torpedoed, injuring several passengers, including two Americans. On April 19, President Wilson delivered an ultimatum to Germany, threatening to sever diplomatic relations with the country unless it ended its submarine warfare.

In 1916, Wilson won the presidential election. Before his inauguration, he pressured the Allies (Great Britain, France, Russia, Serbia, and Japan) and the Central Powers (Germany, Austria-Hungary, Bulgaria, and Turkey) to state their war aims clearly. He also outlined his ideas on how to end the war, which included an international organization that would help guarantee world peace.

▲ A drawing, c.1915, depicts the British ocean liner *Lusitania* being torpedoed.

On February 1, 1917, Germany resumed unrestricted submarine warfare on all allied shipping, and the United States quickly broke off diplomatic relations. The State Department released a telegram that it had intercepted from the German Foreign Secretary Arthur Zimmerman to the German ambassador in Mexico. The secret message proposed that Mexico should ally itself with Germany if the United States entered the war. It also suggested that if Mexico launched a preemptive strike on the United States, it would have Germany's backing and would be rewarded with certain U.S. states if the Central Powers won the war. The message did little to enhance Germany in the eyes of Americans.

THE ZIMMERMAN TELEGRAM: 1917

... We intend to begin unrestricted submarine warfare on the first of February. We shall endeavor in spite of this to keep the United States neutral. In the event of this not succeeding, we make Mexico a proposal of an alliance on the following basis: Make war together, make peace together, generous financial support, and an understanding on our part that Mexico is to reconquer the lost territory in Texas, New Mexico, and Arizona....

THE UNITED STATES ENTERS WORLD WAR I

Sparked by Russian defeats in the war, which led to serious food shortages, Petrograd (now St. Petersburg), the capital, was severely hit by strikes, riots and troop mutinies. Czar Nicholas II abdicated, and a provisional government was formed, but the Bolsheviks, members of a radical left-wing party, were determined to seize power.

Because of this Russian Revolution, President Wilson felt he had greater justification when he asked Congress for a declaration of war against Imperial Germany on April 6. Wilson also knew that, to make the world safe for democracy, the United States would later probably have to send troops into Russia to fight the Communists.

DECLARATION OF WAR AGAINST GERMANY: 1917

... Whereas the Imperial German Government has committed repeated acts of war against the Government and the people of the United States of America, ... a state of war ... which has been thrust upon the United States is formally declared; and ... the President ... is hereby authorized and directed to employ the entire naval and military forces of the United States and the resources of the Government to carry on war against the Imperial German Government....

The first U.S. army units landed in France in June 1917. By September, more than five hundred thousand American troops, known as doughboys, were fighting alongside the Allied armies. These fresh recruits—with more arriving each day—turned the tide of the war. The most significant combat action that American military units saw came in the spring of 1918 when Germany launched several massive attacks in France. The American troops drove the German army back.

World War I was the first war in which airplanes were used in combat. Captain Eddie Rickenbacker was America's greatest ace, having shot down twenty-six enemy aircraft by the end of the war.

An undated photograph of one of the first airplanes used by American flyers in France during World War I. ▶

Benjamin Edgar Cruzan, a bugler with Battery F, 341st Field Artillery, 89th Division, 3rd Army, American Expeditionary Forces, kept a diary. His writing betrayed his third-grade education, but Cruzan had often told his family that he regretted never having asked his father much about his experiences in the Civil War. Cruzan wanted to leave behind a record of his experiences in what at the time was called the "Great War."

BENJAMIN CRUZAN'S DIARY: 1918

... October 23, 1918:

... There was a Raiding party sent out right after our Barrage they Brought Back 28 prisoners and 2 that were badly shot up. they tried to spring something on the Doughs [American soldiers] and they got 2 Hand Grenades in Return Killed one and wound several, 30 of our boys got 30 Fritzys [Germans]....

"... Right after our Barrage they Brought Back 28 prisoners and 2 that were badly shot up...."

November 4, 1918:

Well our Boys went over this Morning the 28 Division a fine Bunch but the attack failed that is as far as we know.... But Maybe Our Boys was only to give a fient attack we heard they advanced 15 kilos on our Left the 92nd Div is to our Right I saw my first German Prisoners I mean Fresh one there were 10, a regular Rocky mts Goats all Beard....

November 11, 1918:

Well now I Guess I am safe to say that the war is over and the only thing Lacking is Signing the peace terms. I am glad to have taken a part in this World War I have spent 1 year and 1 day either in the training camps or on the Route over here and I have spent 53 days on the front. 53 days of actual service on the fireing Line that ant Long but I Can say that I have saw service on the Battle Line....

▲ A 1917 photograph shows French soldiers fighting in the trenches during World World I.

In the autumn of 1918, with its military situation deteriorating, Germany asked for peace with terms based on President Wilson's Fourteen Points—a statement of U.S. war aims that the president had presented to Congress in January 1918. Reluctantly, Great Britain and France agreed, and an armistice was signed on November 11.

Although during the war the Allied leaders had publicly supported Wilson's idealist attitude on how they should behave when the time came for a peace settlement, their national-istic objectives ultimately conflicted with Wilson's altruistic ideas.

The prime minister of France, Georges Clemenceau, demanded not only financial reparations but also territorial concessions from Germany. He insisted that the country be stripped of its military strength so that it could never again wage war. The prime minister of Great Britain, David Lloyd George, wanted to punish Germany for devastating Europe during the war but did not want to utterly destroy the German economy and political system the way Clemenceau and many other people in France did. Unknown to Wilson, several Allied nations had already entered into secret treaties during the war under which they would divide territories taken from the Central Powers. The final terms of the Treaty of Versailles gave them most of what they wanted.

For President Wilson, his Fourteen Points were the only possible program for maintaining a lasting peace in Europe, which he hoped would also ensure a lasting peace for the United States. The first five points covered a broad range of issues in international relations. The next eight points pertained to specific cases of political or territorial readjustments.

WOODROW WILSON'S FOURTEEN POINTS

> "A general association of nations must be formed ... for the purpose of affording mutual guarantees of political independence and territorial integrity to great and small states alike...."

I. Open covenants of peace ...

II. Absolute freedom of navigation upon the seas ...

III. The removal ... of all economic barriers ...

IV. Adequate guarantees given and taken that national armaments will be reduced ...

V. A free, open-minded, and absolutely impartial adjustment of all colonial claims ...

VI. The evacuation of all Russian territory ...

VII. Belgium ... must be evacuated and restored....

VIII. All French territory should be freed and the invaded portions restored, and the wrong done to France by Prussia in 1871 in the matter of Alsace-Lorraine ... should be righted....

IX. A readjustment of the frontiers of Italy should be effected....

X. The people of Austria-Hungary ... should be accorded the freest opportunity to autonomous development....

XI. Rumania, Serbia, and Montenegro should be evacuated....

XII. The Turkish portion of the present Ottoman Empire should be assured a secure sovereignty, but the other nationalities ... now under Turkish rule should be assured ... [the] opportunity of autonomous development....

XIII. An independent Polish state should be erected....

XIV. A general association of nations must be formed under specific covenants for the purpose of affording mutual guarantees of political independence and territorial integrity to great and small states alike....

Wilson thought the last of his points was really the most important one because it called for an "association of nations." Secretly, the allied leaders considered the American president politically naive in the ways of the world, but they also viewed his Fourteen Points as excellent propaganda that would make them look like true statesmen in the eyes of the world. In the end, however, their ambitious but petty postwar plans for their own nations kept them from ever formally adopting the proposals as a basis for peace.

At the war's end, with more than one hundred thousand soldiers dead and over two hundred thousand wounded, America had paid a high price, but there were still other battles to fight. The Bolsheviks (now called Communists) had finally succeeded in overthrowing the short-lived democratic government in Russia in November 1917 and had signed a separate peace treaty with Germany, which took Russia out of the war.

In August 1918, the United States and fourteen other countries sent troops to northern Russia to protect Allied supplies and to support the anticommunist forces in their struggle to retake power from the Communists. The Allied intervention in Russia ended in April 1920. These incursions into Russia were the start of problems that would plague Washington-Moscow relations for decades.

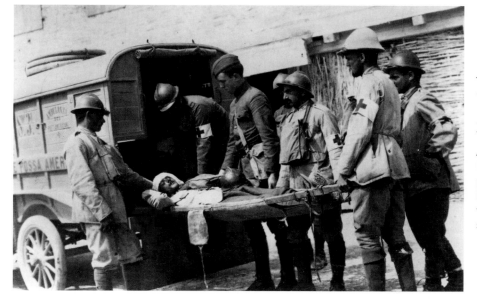

◀ A photograph taken in Italy during World War I shows American Red Cross personnel helping a wounded soldier.

CHAPTER 3

Securing the Peace

1918–1920

The Paris Peace Conference was held from January to June 1919. President Wilson led the American delegation. No prominent Republicans were included, a major political blunder in light of midterm elections. Wilson neglected to build on the support he had during the war from both parties. Instead, in 1918, he campaigned for Democratic candidates. But the Republicans regained control of the House and the Senate, and it was the Senate that would need to ratify the peace treaty.

Although in public, Wilson's Fourteen Points were the starting point for the peace settlement with Germany and its allies, in private the Allies stubbornly resisted Wilson's attempts for a "peace without victory." The victorious Europeans were determined to see that Germany paid a heavy price for the war.

The Big Four—as David Lloyd George of Great Britain, Georges Clemenceau of France, Vittorio Orlando of Italy, and Wilson were called—dominated the proceedings. Leaders from thirty-two nations, representing seventy-five percent of the world's population, attended. Eventually five treaties emerged that dealt with the defeated countries of the Central Powers. They were named after the Paris suburbs of Versailles (Germany), St. Germain (Austria), Trianon (Hungary), Neuilly (Bulgaria), and Serves (Turkey). Since the Versailles Treaty was considered the most important one, that's the name by which the other treaties are known.

▲ A 1919 cartoon shows a perplexed man—the U.S. Senate—looking at the peace treaty that President Wilson has just delivered.

MAJOR TERMS OF THE VERSAILLES TREATY: 1919

1) surrender of all German colonies as League of Nations mandates, 2) return of Alsace-Lorraine to France, 3) "free city" status for Danzig, 4) occupation and special status for the Saarland under French control, 5) demilitarization and a fifteen-year occupation of the Rhineland, 6) reparations of 20,000,000,000 gold German Marks, 7) acceptance of Germany's guilt in causing the war, 8) limitation of Germany's army to 100,000 men, no tanks, no heavy artillery, no poison-gas supplies, no aircraft, and no airships, and 9) limitation of the German Navy to vessels under 100,000 tons, with no submarines.

Edward Mandell House, the son of a Houston, Texas, banker, had already been active in Texas politics for several years when he helped Wilson secure the 1912 Democratic presidential nomination. After Wilson's election, House became the President's closest adviser. President Wilson sent him to Europe in 1914 in an attempt to prevent the outbreak of war and again in 1915 to propose a peace conference.

After the United States entered World War I, House was the American representative at the conference for coordinating Allied activities. He also gathered data for the peace conference, and led the American delegation to draft the Treaty of Versailles and the covenant for a League of Nations.

Although President Wilson respected House's experiences in Europe, the president believed that House's shortcoming was an eagerness to agree with whomever he was talking. Wilson was furious when he realized that House had negotiated away many of the Fourteen Points (while Wilson was back in Washington tending to other matters) in the face of British and French opposition. His sense of House's betrayal was compounded by the first lady, Edith Wilson, who disliked the Texan and had been subtly criticizing House for not having a "very strong character."

For the most part, House thought he was more realistic than President Wilson. Some of the bitterness he felt surfaced in the diary he kept during his stay at the Paris Peace Conference.

EDWARD MANDELL HOUSE'S DIARY: 1919

I am leaving Paris, after eight fateful months, with conflicting emotions. Looking at the conference in retrospect there is much to approve and much to regret. It is easy to say what should have been done, but more difficult to have found a way for doing it.

The bitterness engendered by the war, the hopes raised high in many quarters because of victory, the character of the men having the dominant voices in the making of the Treaty, all had their influence for good or for evil, and were to be reckoned with.

… It may be that Wilson might have had the power and influence if he had remained in Washington and kept clear of the Conference. When he stepped from his lofty pedestal and wrangled with the representatives of other states upon equal terms, he became as common clay.

To those who were saying that the Treaty is bad and should never have been made and that it will involve Europe in infinite difficulties in its enforcement, I feel like admitting it. But I would also say in reply that empires cannot be shattered and new states raised upon their ruins without disturbance. To create new boundaries is always to create new troubles.... While I should have preferred a different peace, I doubt whether it could have been made, for the ingredients for such a peace as I would have had were lacking at Paris.

The same forces that have been at work in the making of this peace would be at work to hinder the enforcement of a different kind of peace, and no one can say with certitude that anything better than has been done could be done at this time. We had to deal with a situation pregnant with difficulties and one which could be met only by an unselfish and idealistic spirit, which was almost wholly absent and which was too much to expect of men come together at such a time and for such a purpose.

And yet I wish we had taken the other road, even if it were less smooth, both now and afterward, than the one we took. We would at least have gone in the right direction and if those who follow us had made it impossible to go the full length of the journey planned, the responsibility would have rested with them and not with us.

THE LEAGUE OF NATIONS

The League of Nations was established on January 25, 1919, by Part I of the Treaty of Versailles. The idea for such a world organization actually originated with British Foreign Secretary Edward Grey. It was enthusiastically adopted by President Woodrow Wilson, who saw it as a means of avoiding future bloodshed. The goals of the organization were to reduce war armaments, to settle disputes between countries, and to secure healthy living conditions for all the people of the world. Wilson saw Article Ten of the League's Covenant as the key to its success because it called on all member nations to preserve the territorial integrity of all other

▲ A 1919 photograph of President and Mrs. Wilson arriving at Versailles for the peace treaty talks.

members. Article Eleven declared that each member nation had the right to advise the League of any circumstances it saw as a threat to war.

COVENANT OF THE LEAGUE OF NATIONS, ARTICLES 10 AND 11: 1919

Article 10. The members of the League undertake to respect and preserve as against external aggression the territorial integrity and existing political independence of all Members of the League. In case of any such aggression or in case of any threat or danger of such aggression the Council shall advise upon the means by which this obligation shall be fulfilled.

Article 11. Any war or threat of war, whether immediately affecting any of the Members of the League or not, is hereby declared a matter of concern to the whole League, and the League shall take any action that may be deemed wise and effectual to safeguard the peace of nations....

RATIFICATION OF THE TREATY

In July 1919, the Treaty of Versailles was submitted to the United States Senate for ratification. At the outset, the members were bitterly divided over the inclusion of the League of Nations. Most Democrats favored immediate ratification. The Irreconcilables, a small group of Republican senators, rejected the treaty entirely because they wanted the United States to stay isolated from the problems of Europe. In the middle were the Reservationists, moderates who favored participation in the League but wanted modifications to protect American interests. They were led by Senator Henry Cabot Lodge, chair of the Foreign Relations Committee, who gave a speech in the Senate on February 28, 1919, in

▲ A portrait, c.1898, of Henry Cabot Lodge, a moderate, who wanted modifications to the Covenant of the League of Nations in order to protect American interests.

which he said he was troubled by the peace treaty, particularly Article Ten of the League Covenant, which required all League members to come

HENRY CABOT LODGE'S SENATE SPEECH: 1919

... In this draft prepared for a constitution of a league of nations ... there is hardly a clause about which men do not already differ.... It seems to have been very hastily drafted, and the result is ... looseness of expression.... We abandon entirely ... the policy laid down by [George] Washington in his Farewell Address and the Monroe doctrine.... Washington declared against permanent alliances.... He did not close the door on temporary alliances for particular purposes.... Under the terms of this league draft ... the Monroe doctrine disappears. It has been our cherished guide and guard [in foreign policy] for nearly a century.... Under this draft of the constitution of the league of nations, American questions and European questions and Asian and African questions are all alike put within the control and jurisdiction of the league. Europe will have the right to take part in the settlement of all American questions.... For this reason I ask the press and the public, and, of course, the Senate, to consider well the gravity of this proposition before it....

to the aid of any member country under attack. He felt that the organization would threaten the sovereignty of the United States by binding it to international commitments that it would not or could not keep.

When President Wilson failed to persuade the Senate to ratify the treaty, he embarked on an arduous speaking tour of the country in September 1919 in the hope that public opinion would put enough pressure on senators to support ratification. But the trip soon began to take its toll on his health. On October 2, he suffered a massive stroke. Although Wilson's health eventually improved, he never fully recovered.

WOODROW WILSON'S SPEECH IN INDIANAPOLIS: 1919

... You have heard a great deal about Article X of the Covenant of the League of Nations. Article X speaks the conscience of the world.... We are absolutely discredited if we fought this war and then neglect the essential safeguard against it....

There is not an oppressed people in the world which cannot get a hearing at [the League of Nations], and you know, my fellow citizens, what a hearing will mean if the cause of those people is just. The one thing which those people have reason to dread, have most reason to dread, is publicity and discussion, because if you are challenged to give a reason why you are doing a wrong that it has to be an exceedingly good reason, and if you give a bad reason you confess judgment, and the opinion of mankind goes against you....

The Treaty of Versailles was presented to the full Senate in November 1919. It contained fourteen amendments. The most important one limited the obligations of the United States under Article Ten by requiring congressional approval of any action. President Wilson refused to accept the changes and told the Senate Democrats to vote with the Republican Irreconcilables to defeat Senator Lodge and his supporters. Although the treaty did eventually get the support of a majority of the senators, it failed to receive the two-thirds vote needed for ratification. As a result, the United States entered into separate peace treaties with Germany and the other Central Powers. It never did join the League of Nations, a move which many historians think weakened the organization and contributed to World War II by leaving it unable to prevent the fascist governments of Germany, Italy, and Japan to come to power.

WOMEN WIN THE RIGHT TO VOTE

The Nineteenth Amendment to the Constitution, which guarantees American women the right to vote was first introduced in Congress in 1878. Supporters of voting rights for women worked tirelessly to achieve their goal, and only a few of the early supporters lived to see the final victory in 1920.

Militant suffragists used tactics such as parades, silent vigils, and hunger strikes and were heckled, jailed, and sometimes physically abused by opponents. By 1918, President Wilson had changed his position on this matter, and he now supported the amendment.

On May 21, 1919, the House of Representatives passed the amendment, and two weeks later, the Senate followed. On August 18, 1920, Tennessee became the thirty-sixth state to ratify the amendment. It now had the necessary support of three-fourths of the states.

NINETEENTH AMENDMENT: 1920

… The right of the citizens of the United States to vote shall not be denied or abridged by the United States or any State on account of sex.

… Congress shall have power to enforce this article by appropriate legislation….

Help us to win the vote

◄ A suffragist in 1914 carries a sign at a rally to help women win the right to vote.

not only caused family violence and poverty but also was a sin. Carrie Nation was one of the most famous early prohibitionists. Even though the sale of liquor was illegal in Kansas, where she lived, the saloons ignored the law. Nation traveled across the state harassing customers, threatening bartenders, and hacking liquor crates to pieces with her hatchet.

With the ratification of the Eighteenth Amendment on January 16, 1919, prohibition was the law of the land. Unfortunately, it presented lucrative opportunities for illegal activities. By the end of the decade, the importation, manufacture, and distribution of alcoholic beverages was largely in the hands of criminals and illegal home manufacturers.

PROHIBITION ERA

The prohibition movement—a campaign against liquor—started in the early 1800s, when alcohol consumption was at an all-time high, but because its production was one of the nation's most important industries, government leaders paid little attention to what people were saying. During the next several decades, however, clergymen and female reformers began to spread the message that drinking

EIGHTEENTH AMENDMENT: 1919

... After one year from the ratification of this article, the manufacture, sale, or transportation of intoxicating liquors within, the importation thereof into, or the exportation thereof from the United States and all territory subject to the jurisdiction thereof for beverage purposes is hereby prohibited....

CHAPTER 4

The Roaring Twenties

1920–1929

The Great War was over, and American troops had returned from Europe victorious. Now the country was ready to celebrate. The "Roaring Twenties" and the "Jazz Age" were two names that people called the decade of the 1920s.

PROBLEMS OF PROHIBITION

Prohibition, the national ban on alcohol, went into effect at the beginning of the 1920s, but it didn't stop people from drinking. Some people made their own liquor, which was called bathtub gin, because it was usually made in a bathtub! Most alcohol was smuggled into the United States from either Mexico or Canada.

Criminal gangs, like Al Capone's in Chicago, soon took over selling liquor and fought whiskey wars to gain control of the different sections of the city or the state. They often resorted to murder to get what they wanted. On April 27, 1926, Capone and members of his gang used a machine gun to kill an assistant state's attorney—William H. McSwiggin—in Chicago. *The Chicago Daily Tribune* reported the incident.

ARTICLE FROM *THE CHICAGO DAILY TRIBUNE*: 1926

William H. McSwiggin, youthful assistant state's attorney, who was known as "the hanging prosecutor" because of his success in the conduct of murder trials, was shot to death last night when a machine gunner ... poured a blast of fire upon him and two other men....

Chief of Police [Morgan] Collins sent every available policeman.... He said ... "The gangs that deal in booze become increasingly dangerous.... We shall stay at it until we have cleaned up the remnants of these gangs."

▲ Following a raid during the prohibition era in the 1920s, agents pour illegal barrels of liquor down the sewer.

THE JAZZ AGE AND FLAPPERS

Jazz was the music of the era. Created by African American musicians in New Orleans in the early 1900s, the music spread north with the black migration of the 1920s. Musicians like Louis Armstrong and "Duke" Ellington played it in nightclubs like Harlem's Cotton Club in New York City. The Cotton Club was a legal nightclub, but millions of others were not. They were called speakeasies, where patrons could buy any type of liquor they wanted.

As jazz music developed, so did wild new dances, such as the Charleston. Clothing styles also changed. Some young women, called flappers, started wearing skirts so short they shocked older Americans. "Texas" Guinan was the most famous flapper. With her outrageous personality and her famous quips, Guinan (born Mary Louise Cecilia in Waco, Texas) brought in more customers than any other speakeasy hostess during Prohibition.

The Coming of the Automobile

Americans started buying everything in sight, and their debts rose steadily, made possible by a new kind of buying. Before World War I, Americans paid for everything in cash, except perhaps their homes. Now, people were encouraged to use the installment plan, which meant they could buy it now and pay it off in small amounts over a period of time.

The most important new product of the day was the automobile. When it was invented in the late 1800s, the automobile was handmade and expensive. Only rich people could afford to buy one. Henry Ford changed all that. By using assembly-line production, he reduced the time it took to make a car, which drastically lowered the price. The automobile allowed people to move farther and farther from where they worked, so that they could now buy homes in the suburbs and drive to their city jobs.

Radio and Movies

If the automobile helped Americans see more of the world, radio brought the world to them. On November 2, 1920, KDKA went on the air in Pittsburgh, Pennsylvania. Soon stations all over the country were broadcasting news, concerts, and popular series like *Amos 'n' Andy*. Sports were among the most popular radio broadcasts. "Babe" Ruth thrilled audiences with his home runs, and Jack Dempsey and Gene Tunney kept listeners tuned in with their boxing matches. Unlike in Europe, where radio stations were owned by the government, people listened in the United States to privately owned networks like NBC and CBS.

The Great Train Robbery, produced in 1903, was the first full-length movie. Soon millions of Americans started attending "picture shows." These early films were silent, but in 1927, the first "talkie" was released: *The Jazz Singer*, starring Al Jolson. Within a couple of years, almost every movie had sound.

▲ The assembly line allowed automobiles to be made faster and, in turn, cost less.

PRESIDENTS OF THE 1920S

The stroke which President Wilson suffered in 1919 rendered him an invalid. For the rest of his term in office, he was capable of doing only the simplest presidential tasks.

On March 4, 1921, Wilson attended Republican President-elect Warren G. Harding's inauguration, and for the next three years, Wilson and his wife lived quietly in Washington, D.C. He died on February 3, 1924.

During the 1920s, the United States witnessed the greatest burst of prosperity in its history, and most Americans began to enjoy a standard of living that was higher than previous generations. Three consecutive Republican presidents took credit for the good times: Warren G. Harding, Calvin Coolidge, and Herbert Hoover.

Harding's campaign slogan was "A Return to Normalcy," and it was a perfect description of American politics for the entire decade. The average citizen was tired of the reforming zeal that characterized the Progressive Era and of the moral vision of Wilson's wartime government. What Americans wanted was an administration whose domestic economic policies opposed government interference in their lives and encouraged business expansion. In his inaugural address, President Harding told the American people that this was what he wanted, too.

HARDING'S INAUGURAL ADDRESS: 1921

... We can reduce the abnormal expenditures, and we will. We can strike at war taxation, and we must. We must face the grim necessity, with full knowledge that the task is to be solved.... Our most dangerous tendency is to expect too much of government, and at the same time do for it too little. We contemplate the immediate task of putting our public household in order. We need a rigid and yet sane economy, combined with fiscal justice, and it must be attended by individual prudence and thrift, which are so essential to this trying hour and reassuring for the future....

... I pledge an administration wherein all the agencies of Government are called to serve, and ever promote an understanding of Government purely as an expression of the popular will....

Harding was friendly and popular and his administration helped streamline federal spending with the Budget and Accounting Act of 1921, but it was also rocked by major scandals involving some of the members of the president's cabinet.

Harding died in 1923 while on a trip out West, and his vice president, Calvin Coolidge, became president. By launching an immediate investigation of the corruption of Harding's administration, Coolidge quickly won the confidence of the American people, who admired his courage and personal integrity. He also continued Harding's fiscal policies by reducing government debt and letting business have free rein in the pursuit of profits.

Coolidge was so successful in removing the stigma of corruption from the Republican party and in associating his administration with the prosperity of the times that he was the unanimous choice of the delegates to the party's national convention in 1924. The day before the election, President Coolidge addressed the nation, telling people that it was their obligation as Americans to learn the issues of the election and then get out and vote.

COOLIDGE'S ADDRESS ON "THE DUTIES OF CITIZENSHIP": 1924

… To live up to the full measure of citizenship in this nation requires not only action, but it requires intelligent action. It is necessary to secure information and to acquire education. The background of our citizenship is the meeting house and the school house, the place of religious worship, and the place of intellectual training. But we cannot abandon our education at the school house door. We have to keep it up through life. A political campaign can be justified only on the grounds that it enables the citizens to become informed as to what policies are best for themselves and for their country, in order that they may vote to elect those who from their past record and present professions they know will put such policies into effect. The purpose of a campaign is to send an intelligent and informed voter to the ballot box. All the speeches, all the literature, all the organization, all the effort, all the time and all the money, which are not finally registered on election day, are wasted….

When President Coolidge decided not to run for a second term, the Republicans nominated Herbert Hoover, who was Secretary of Commerce. The country was still riding the high tide of prosperity that the Republicans took full credit for.

In a speech that closed his 1928 presidential campaign, Hoover, a self-made millionaire, expressed the view that the American way of life was based on rugged individualism and self-reliance. He also felt the federal government, which had assumed unprecedented economic powers, should shrink back to its pre–World War I size to avoid interfering with business. Hoover won by a landslide.

▲ Herbert Hoover addresses a crowd at Madison Square Garden in New York City during his campaign for the presidency.

HOOVER'S "RUGGED INDIVIDUALISM" CAMPAIGN SPEECH: 1928

... When the war [World War I] closed, the most vital of all issues both in our own country and throughout the world was whether government should continue their wartime ownership and operation of many instrumentalities of production and distribution. We were challenged with a peace-time choice between the American system of rugged individualism and a European philosophy of ... paternalism and state socialism. The acceptance of these ideas would have ... meant the undermining of the individual initiative and enterprise through which our people have grown to unparalleled greatness....

The Red Scare

In the first years after World War I, the nation experienced an hysteria known as the "Red Scare." The success of the 1917 Communist revolution in Russia convinced many Americans that the "Reds"—as they were commonly known because of the color of their flag—and their sympathizers were going to try to take over governments elsewhere in the world, including the United States. In 1919, state and federal law enforcement agencies arrested more than four thousand suspected Communists.

To many Americans, the Red Scare, combined with labor unrest at home, was proof that their country was also on the verge of a revolution. In 1919 alone, there were thousands of strikes, involving four million workers.

Americans blamed foreigners for most of these problems. In 1921, Congress passed the Quota Act, which set the maximum number of immigrants who could enter the United States at three hundred fifty thousand. The National Origins Act of 1924 further reduced the number of entering immigrants.

Sacco and Vanzetti Trial

This bias against people who were not born in the United States also manifested itself in the trial of Nicola Sacco and Bartolomeo Vanzetti. They were Italian-born and admitted anarchists. In July 1921, a jury in Massachusetts found them guilty of robbery and murder.

They were sentenced to death, but there were many people who felt that the two men had been convicted because of their political beliefs rather than by the evidence presented. By August 22, 1927, all of their appeals

▲ This 1927 photograph shows Vanzetti (left) and Sacco (right) handcuffed together as they enter the courthouse.

had been exhausted, and their execution was set for the following day. With only a few hours left to live, Vanzetti wrote a letter to Sacco's son, Dante, expressing his hope that, one day, Americans would reappraise their fears of radical beliefs and of those who held them.

LETTER FROM BARTOLOMEO VANZETTI TO DANTE SACCO WHILE IN DEATH HOUSE: 1927

My dear Dante:

I still hope, and we will fight until the last moment, to revindicate our right to live and to be free, but all the forces of the State and of the money and reaction are deadly against us because we are libertarians or anarchists....

But, if you do well, you will grow and understand your father's and my case and your father's and my principles, for which we will soon be put to death....

Some day you will understand ... [that] your father has sacrificed everything dear and sacred to the human heart and soul for his fate [sic] in liberty and justice for all. That day you will be proud of your father, and if you come brave enough, you will take his place in the struggle between tyranny and liberty and you will vindicate his [our] names and our blood....

Remember, Dante, remember always these things; we are not criminals; they convicted us on a frame-up; they denied us a new trial; and if we will be executed after seven years, four months, and seventeen days of unspeakable tortures and wrong, it is for what I have already told you; because we were for the poor and against the exploitation and oppression of the man by the man....

The day will come when you will understand the atrocious cause of the above written words, in all its fullness. Then you will honor us....

> **"**... if we will be executed ... it is ... because we were for the poor and against the exploitation and oppression of the man by the man....**"**

KU KLUX KLAN REVIVED

The Ku Klux Klan, a white-suprem-acist organization formed after the Civil War, saw a revival of its influ-ence in the 1920s. It drew most of its membership from the rural areas and small towns of the South and Midwest. Originally, the Klan only opposed African Americans, but during the 1920s, it added Catholics, Jews, and foreigners to the people it considered unworthy of being called "Americans."

Some members of the Klan parti-cipated in what was known as "night riding," where they dressed in their robes and hoods and drove all over the countryside, trying to intimidate people they thought had no business living in the United States. Often, these rides would end with mem-bers of the Klan forcibly removing men or boys from their homes to be whipped, hanged, or burned at the stake.

Hiram Evans joined the Ku Klux Klan in 1920 and led Klansmen in acts of violence against people they hated. In November 1922, Evans became the Klan's Imperial Wizard, its highest-ranking official. Under his leadership, the organization grew rapidly, and in the 1920s Klansmen were elected to positions of political power in several states, including Texas, Oklahoma, Indiana, Oregon, and Maine. By 1925, the membership had reached four million. The Klan spread its message through its own publications, such as *The Good Citizen*. After 1925, membership in the Klan declined rapidly not only because of scandals involving its leadership but also because of opposition from Americans who would no longer tolerate such bigotry.

EVANS'S MESSAGE IN *THE GOOD CITIZEN*: 1924

... Notwithstanding the sacrifices that had to be made ... [by] our young men who crossed the sea and laid down their lives on the battlefields of the Old World, it has taken the Ku Klux Klan to awaken even a portion of the population of the United States to our national peril. Our religious and political foes are not only within our gates, but are coming by the hundreds of thousands, bringing the chaos and ruin of old European and Asiatic countries to un-Americanize and destroy our nation....

THE SCOPES TRIAL

Church attendance began to decline in the 1920s, and fundamentalist Protestants fought back against the ever-growing secular culture. They believed Darwin's theory of evolution was a symbol of what was wrong with American society and demanded a literal interpretation of the Bible.

Several state legislatures passed laws that prohibited the teaching of evolution, which stated that human beings had evolved from lower forms of life—such as monkeys and apes—rather than being descendants of Adam and Eve. John Scopes, a young high-school biology teacher, challenged Tennessee's law, and he was put on trial. To defend him, the American Civil Liberties Union brought in Clarence Darrow, the most famous defense lawyer in the country. The World Christian Fundamentalist Union brought in William Jennings Bryan to assist the prosecution. H. L. Mencken, a prominent journalist, book reviewer, and political commentator, attended the trial and wrote an account of it.

H. L. MENCKEN'S ACCOUNT OF "THE MONKEY TRIAL": 1925

July 11

The selection of a jury to try Scopes, which went on all yesterday afternoon in the atmosphere of a blast furnace, showed to what extreme length the salvation of the local primates has been pushed. It was obvious after a few rounds that the jury would be unanimously hot for Genesis....

July 14

[Clarence Darrow's great speech yesterday] rose like a wind and ended like a flourish of bugles.... But the morons in the audience, when it was over, simply hissed it. During the whole time of its delivery ... Bryan sat tight-lipped and unmoved....

July 18

Darrow has lost this case. It was lost long before he came to Dayton [Tennessee]. But it seems to me that he has nevertheless performed a great public service by fighting it....

Although John Scopes was convicted—clearly he had broken Tennessee's anti-evolution statute—and was fined one hundred dollars, modernists claimed victory. The weaknesses of Christian beliefs in opposition to modern discoveries in science were challenged, and thereafter the over-bearing influence that religious fundamentalists had on state education, especially in the South, began a steady decline.

Clarence Darrow, *(left)* and William Jennings Bryan *(right)* are shown in the courtroom during the Scopes trial of 1925. ▶

FOREIGN POLICY IN THE 1920s

Although the United States did not join the League of Nations, its foreign policy was far from being isolationist. In the 1920s, in an effort to show the rest of the world that it had no intention of withdrawing from the world scene, the United States participated in the signing of several treaties.

The Five-Power Treaty was signed in 1922 at the Washington Armament Conference. It limited the tonnage of navies. The Nine-Power Treaty was also signed at the same conference. The signatories pledged to respect the territorial integrity of China. In 1927, when civil war broke out in Nicaragua, President Coolidge sent in American troops. In 1927, when President Coolidge gave his State of the Union address, he showed clearly that the main foreign policy objective of the United States was world peace.

COOLIDGE'S STATE OF THE UNION ADDRESS: 1927

... We were confronted by [a] similar condition on a small scale in Nicaragua. Our marine and naval forces protected our citizens and their property and prevented a heavy sacrifice of life and the destruction of that country by a reversion to a state of revolution.... This was done on the assurance that we would cooperate in restoring a state of peace where our rights would be protected by giving our assistance in the conduct of the next presidential election [in Nicaragua], which occurs in a few months. With this assurance the population returned to their peacetime pursuits, with the exception of some small roving bands of outlaws....

"Our marine and naval forces protected our citizens and their property...."

During the Hoover administration, there was a shift in American foreign policy. The government decided that the Monroe Doctrine could not be used to justify American intervention in the Western Hemisphere.

BLACK TUESDAY

At home, the country's economic situation still seemed on the surface to be good, but there were, in fact, plenty of warning signs that people ignored. For one thing, crop prices fell throughout the period, and corporations were making huge profits, but their workers weren't always sharing in them. More and more people were going deeper in debt each year. By 1927, consumer spending and housing construction were down, and workers were being laid off.

All this time, while the economy was getting weaker, the stock market was skyrocketing. People were borrowing money to take their chances on Wall Street. Stock prices kept going up, and investors thought they could pay back their loans with the profits they made off their stocks.

On "Black Tuesday"—October 29, 1929—the bubble burst. In just a few weeks, stock values fell over thirty billion dollars. Millions of people went broke. Companies began laying off workers, and the economy went into a downward spiral, marking the start of the worst depression in American history.

TIME LINE

1900	▪ President McKinley is reelected.
1901	▪ President McKinley is assassinated and is succeeded by Vice President Theodore Roosevelt, the twenty-sixth U.S. president.
1903	▪ The Wright Brothers make their first flight at Kitty Hawk.
1908	▪ William Howard Taft is elected the twenty-seventh U.S. president.
1909	▪ Robert Peary reaches the North Pole.
1911	▪ The Triangle Shirtwaist Company fire in New York City exposes unsafe factory conditions.
1912	▪ Woodrow Wilson is elected the twenty-eighth U.S. president.
1914	▪ The Panama Canal is completed and opens to traffic.
1915	▪ German submarines sink the British ocean liner *Lusitania*.
1917	▪ The United States enters World War I.
1918	▪ Armistice ending World War I is signed.
1919	▪ The Treaty of Versailles, outlining terms for peace at the end of World War I, is rejected by the U.S. Senate.
1919	▪ The Eighteenth Amendment to the Constitution is ratified.
1920	▪ The Nineteenth Amendment to the Constitution is ratified, granting women the right to vote.
1920	▪ Warren G. Harding is elected the twenty-ninth U.S. president.
1921	▪ President Harding signs a resolution declaring peace with Austria and Germany.
1921	▪ Bias against immigrants is manifested in the Sacco and Vanzetti trial.
1923	▪ President Harding dies suddenly and is succeeded by his vice president, Calvin Coolidge, who becomes the thirtieth U.S. president.
1925	▪ Tennessee passes a law against the teaching of evolution in public schools; John Scopes goes on trial for teaching evolution.
1929	▪ The stock market crashes, precipitating the Great Depression.

GLOSSARY

ace: military pilot who has shot down a lot of enemy planes.

altruistic: being motivated by a sincere concern for others.

anarchists: persons who believe in political disorder.

armistice: stoppage of military battles by mutual agreement.

assembly line: line of factory workers putting together consecutive pieces of a machine.

bathtub gin: illegal alcoholic beverages often made in bathtubs.

Bolsheviks: participants in the Russian Revolution.

Communists: people who believe that a nation, not individuals, should own everything.

depression: period of decline in a nation's economy.

doughboys: American nickname for soldiers in World War I.

evolution: theory that living things change with the passage of time and differ from their ancestors.

exploitation: taking advantage of a person or a country.

federal reserve banks: U.S. government banks that lend money to regular banks.

flappers: young women in the 1920s interested mainly in having a good time.

fundamentalist: person who interprets the Bible literally.

injunctions: court orders that keep people from doing certain things.

installment plan: paying for merchandise over a period of time.

isolationist: position of a person who doesn't believe in having political agreements with other countries.

jazz: American music started by black bands in the 1920s.

muckrakers: writers who expose alleged corruption by government or business officials.

national parks: land set aside by the government for recreational purposes.

naturalist: person interested in preserving a nation's plants and animals.

prohibition: the outlawing of alcoholic beverages.

propaganda: the systematic promotion of information to advance one's cause.

reparations: financial compensation paid by a country defeated in war for economic losses suffered by the victorious nation.

Red Scare: fear in the 1920s that there would be a Communist revolution in the United States.

signatories: persons who sign a treaty or other document.

speakeasies: illegal nightclubs during the 1920s.

suffragists: persons who think a woman should have the right to vote.

FURTHER INFORMATION

BOOKS

Busby, Peter. *First to Fly: How Wilbur and Orville Wright Invented the Airplane.* Crown Books for Young Readers, 2003.

Keegan, John. *An Illustrated History of the First World War*. Alfred A. Knopf, 2001.

Moran, Jeffrey P. *The Scopes Trial: A Brief History with Documents*. Bedford/St. Martin's Press, 2002.

WEB SITES

www.worldwar1.com/reflib.htm The name of this Web site is Trenches on the Web, and it presents a comprehensive look at World War I with sections on maps, documents, photos, and more.

www.hoover.archives.gov/exhibits/Hooverstory/gallery03/gallery03.html This Web site focuses on the era of the Roaring Twenties and is part of the Herbert Hoover Presidential Library and Museum. It presents a summary of this decade with interesting pieces on prohibition, fads and sports of the era, and much more.

USEFUL ADDRESS

The Henry Ford [museum]
20900 Oakwood Blvd.
Dearborn, MI 48124
Telephone: (313) 982-6100

★★★ INDEX ★★★